T0088309

John Rutter

Lo, how a Rose e'er blooming

(*Es ist ein' Ros' entsprungen*)

Oboe and piano

OXFORD

Lo, how a Rose e'er blooming

(Es ist ein' Ros' entsprungen)

JOHN RUTTER
based on a German chorale melody

© Collegium Music Publications 2022. Exclusively licensed worldwide to Oxford University Press.

Printed in Great Britain

OXFORD UNIVERSITY PRESS MUSIC DEPARTMENT, GREAT CLARENDON STREET, OXFORD OX2 6DP
The Moral Rights of the Arranger have been asserted. Photocopying this copyright material is ILLEGAL.

18
pp
mp
poco cresc.
mp
cresc.
24
mf
p
mf
p
30
poco largamente
mp
mf
f
cresc.
mf
f
36
a tempo
mp
mp
mp

42
p
p
47
poco rit.
a tempo, poco più tranquillo
mp
p
p molto legato e dolce
53
mp
cresc.
mp
58
rall.
dim.
p
dim.
p

OBOE

Lo, how a Rose e'er blooming

(Es ist ein' Ros' entsprungen)

JOHN RUTTER

based on a German chorale melody

© Collegium Music Publications 2022. Exclusively licensed worldwide to Oxford University Press.

Printed in Great Britain

OXFORD UNIVERSITY PRESS MUSIC DEPARTMENT, GREAT CLARENDON STREET, OXFORD OX2 6DP

The Moral Rights of the Arranger have been asserted. Photocopying this copyright material is ILLEGAL.